CCSS **Genre** Folktale

MW00907192

Essential Question
What are some messages in animal stories?

THE WINGS OF THE BUTTERFLY

by Julia Wall
illustrated by Pamela Becker

CHAPTER 1

Chimidyue Is Lost

Once a young girl named Chimidyue (*chim-ID-yoo-ah*) lived near the Amazon River with her parents, sisters, aunts, and cousins in a large house called a maloca (*mul-OH-kah*). The maloca was in a beautiful clearing filled with the sound of chattering birds, but as Chimidyue grew older, she became increasingly curious about the nearby rain forest.

She imagined exploring the forest and the looks on her friends' faces when she returned and told them, "Wait till you hear what I've been doing!"

An opportunity for adventure soon came Chimidyue's way. Late one warm afternoon, she was making baskets with her mother and aunts when a blue morpho butterfly with dazzling light-blue wings attracted her attention.

"Look!" Chimidyue exclaimed, but the women glanced up only briefly, their hands still working furiously. The butterfly was a welcome distraction for Chimidyue. She hated the boring work of weaving baskets.

Chimidyue's baskets were usually full of holes and the patterns crooked because she was "all fingers and thumbs." Her family affectionately called her "Little Thumb," because no matter how many times Chimidyue was shown the correct technique for basket making, her baskets were never evenly woven.

The basket Chimidyue was working on lay forgotten in her lap; she was mesmerized by the flight of the butterfly as its wings caught the sun's rays. It hovered close to Chimidyue as if sensing her interest.

"Get back to work, Chimidyue," instructed her mother.

Chimidyue pretended that she hadn't heard. Once her mother's eyes had returned to her own basket, Chimidyue placed her half-finished one gently on the ground and rose to her feet.

The butterfly was moving away from her now, as if it wanted Chimidyue to follow. Chimidyue began to imitate its flight, waving her arms in the gentle breeze.

Her mother spoke more sharply this time. "Please sit down and finish your basket, Chimidyue."

With a loud sigh, Chimidyue did as she was told. Forcing her attention back to her basket, she watched the butterfly out of the corner of her eye.

Now it was hovering again, like it was waiting, and Chimidyue had an idea. "I'm going to get a drink," she said, hoping that the butterfly would head in the direction of the maloca.

As if it had understood her, the butterfly did just that, and Chimidyue quietly padded after it, trying not to attract attention. Once they had reached the back of the maloca, she peeked around the side, but not one of the women looked up.

"Butterfly, where are you taking me?" asked Chimidyue. But the butterfly said nothing. It just flew toward the forest.

For a moment, Chimidyue felt torn. She longed to follow, but she knew she would be in big trouble when she returned. And what if the elders' stories were true? What if there really were creatures in the forest that could transform into something else?

"It can't be true," Chimidyue thought. She imagined how she would be the center of attention when she came back, and with that thought she set off after the butterfly, which had already flown ahead. "Wait!" Chimidyue whispered fiercely, and it seemed as if the butterfly did, hovering until she caught up.

Chimidyue hadn't gone far when she felt as if the forest had swallowed her whole. She glanced behind her, but she could no longer see the maloca.

"Butterfly!" Chimidyue called. "How will I find my way back?" She stopped. The butterfly had disappeared—and Chimidyue realized she was alone in the forest, with night falling fast. "Butterfly!" she cried. "Where are you?"

The Talking Birds

Chimidyue's heart seemed to beat more loudly than the birdsong as she hurried in what she thought was the direction of the maloca. After a couple of minutes, she suspected she was walking even deeper into the forest. She had no idea which direction was home.

Sobbing and panic-stricken, Chimidyue would have given anything at that moment to be back with her mother and aunts, finishing off her basket.

Chop, chop. Chop, chop. Chimidyue thought she must be dreaming—it sounded like an ax chopping wood! Why would someone be chopping wood in the middle of the forest when it was getting dark? "What does it matter?" Chimidyue wondered. "Someone is here, and they might be able to help me."

She followed the sound and thought she glimpsed a man in the distance, chopping down a tree.

Chimidyue started to run toward the man, nearly twisting her ankle on a tree root in her hurry to reach him. "Hello!" she called as she ran so that he wouldn't be startled when she appeared before him. "Hello!"

Chimidyue burst into a clearing, but instead of a person, a woodpecker was tap-tap-tapping on a tree.

"Oh! I thought you were a human!" said Chimidyue. She rubbed her eyes; she must have been seeing things.

"Why am I talking to a bird?" she thought. "It's not as if it can reply!"

To her astonishment, the woodpecker responded. "Why would I want to be a human?" it snapped angrily.

"Oh, no," thought Chimidyue. "The elders' stories are true—mysterious things really *do* happen in the forest. If only I'd believed them and remained at home!"

Even though Chimidyue felt ridiculous having a conversation with a bird, she decided to reply. "I wanted you to be a human," she explained, "so that you could show me the way home."

"I could show you the way," said the woodpecker, "but I'm too busy. You humans think animals exist only to assist you. Well, not this one!" And it flew off.

"Wait!" cried Chimidyue, but the woodpecker had vanished.

Chimidyue continued walking. She soon discovered a maloca similar to her home. "Someone will be inside," she assured herself, "and they will help me."

Sure enough, Chimidyue could see an elderly woman busily weaving a hammock, and her heart soared. "I'm so glad I've found you because I'm completely lost."

The moment Chimidyue stepped closer to the maloca, its roof began to flap as though it were caught in a hurricane.

"What's happening?" yelled Chimidyue in alarm.

The maloca and the elderly woman rose into the air. "Come back!" Chimidyue shouted, but they had disappeared into the treetops. All Chimidyue could see now was a toucan, which settled itself huffily on a branch before screeching and flying off.

CHAPTER 3

Meeting the Monkeys

Chimidyue trudged on through the forest, growing increasingly weary. She realized how hungry she was when a fruit dropped to the ground in front of her. She picked it up and devoured it, and when another one landed on the ground, Chimidyue devoured that, too. "Maybe I'd better control my greed," she thought. "This may be the only food I find for a while." Just then, another fruit dropped.

"What's happening?" Chimidyue wondered. She heard leaves rustling, and suddenly a spider monkey's face appeared in front of her. "So you're the one dropping fruit!" exclaimed Chimidyue.

As soon as she spoke, several spider monkeys clambered to the ground and transformed into women. This time, Chimidyue wasn't surprised—this was the third occasion she had observed animals or humans changing their form.

One of the women turned to Chimidyue. "We hear that you followed a butterfly and have gotten lost in the forest," she said. Chimidyue nodded. "It's late and dark now, but we'll show you the way home tomorrow," the woman said sympathetically.

"Thank you!" replied Chimidyue. "But where will I sleep tonight?"

"Come with us," the woman instructed her. "We live nearby with the King of the Monkeys."

Chimidyue followed the woman to a large maloca and was introduced to the king, who was stretched out in a hammock and wearing a gold crown. "What's this girl doing here?" he demanded.

"She's lost," replied the woman nervously, "and tomorrow, we're taking her home to her family."

The Monkey King grunted and dismissed them with his hand.

Chimidyue watched the other women, who were tidying the maloca after eating their evening meal. Their clothing, made of fabric decorated with paint and feathers, shone in the firelight.

"Those baskets look just like the ones we make in our village," Chimidyue exclaimed.

"I make them, too," Chimidyue continued, "but I'm not a skilled basket maker. My family calls me Little Thumb."

"You're honest to admit that," replied one of the women. "Sit with me, and I will teach you how to improve your technique."

Chimidyue really wasn't interested in weaving a basket, but she didn't want to upset her new friend either, so she listened while the woman patiently explained how to weave the fibers together. It was an explanation Chimidyue had heard dozens of times before, but this time, it seemed different.

"The secret to a well-made basket," the woman explained, "is patience and a good attitude. If you start sighing and are impatient, you'll never make a strong and beautiful basket."

"It's as if she already knows me," thought Chimidyue. She relaxed and started to weave the fibers carefully. Her finished basket wasn't perfect, but it was a big improvement from those she'd woven with her mother and aunts.

"Thank you," said Chimidyue, yawning. "Can I take this home with me?" The woman agreed, then showed her to a hammock, where she settled herself and was soon fast asleep.

CHAPTER 4
Finding the Way Home

As Chimidyue slept, she dreamed that the Monkey King had transformed into a jaguar. She woke with a fright to hear a voice saying, "I want to eat Chimidyue."

"What are you saying?" she shouted fearfully.

"What? Who's talking to me?" mumbled the Monkey King, still half asleep.

"It's me, Chimidyue. You said you want to eat me!"

"Now, why would I say that?" replied the Monkey King indignantly. "Monkeys don't eat humans!" Soon he was snoring loudly once again.

Chimidyue closed her eyes, but she couldn't sleep, and again she heard, "I want to eat Chimidyue."

She stared at the Monkey King's hammock, and in the dim light she realized that the Monkey King had transformed into a jaguar!

Chimidyue climbed out of her hammock, grabbed her basket, and sprinted through the forest. "That dream saved my life!" she thought.

At that moment, Chimidyue realized that no one would believe all the incredible things that had happened to her.

When she was certain she wasn't being followed, Chimidyue stopped to rest under the branches of a kapok tree. Hugging her basket to her chest, Chimidyue began to cry hot, salty tears. "I hate this forest!" she sobbed noisily.

"Why is that?" requested a tiny voice.

Chimidyue looked up. On a branch of the kapok tree was the largest blue morpho butterfly she'd ever seen.

"Hello," sniffed Chimidyue. "Maybe you can explain to me why everything in this forest keeps changing."

"The forest is different from your world," the butterfly replied. "Things don't always stay the same."

"Next time, I'll make sure I tell someone where I'm going," said Chimidyue.

"Come with me, and I'll show you the way home," said the butterfly.

Chimidyue followed the butterfly through the rain forest, and they eventually arrived at the wide banks of the Amazon River. Far in the distance, on the other side, was her maloca. "How did I cross the river to this side?" she asked in surprise. "I don't remember doing that."

"Nothing is impossible," the butterfly replied.

That didn't explain anything, but Chimidyue sensed this would be all she was told. "How will I get across?"

"Close your eyes," instructed the butterfly, so Chimidyue did, and she began to feel as light and graceful as a morpho butterfly.

"Oh!" said Chimidyue when she opened her eyes a few moments later. She was on the riverbank near her home. Her mother was standing on the path ahead of her, anxiously scanning the wide riverbank for her missing daughter.

"Thank you!" Chimidyue called gratefully to the butterfly, and she ran toward her mother. "Mom, Mom!" she yelled at the top of her voice "You can't call me Little Thumb anymore!"

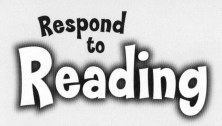

Respond to Reading

Summarize

Use details from *The Wings of the Butterfly* to summarize the story. Your graphic organizer may help you.

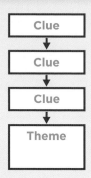

Text Evidence

1. What features help you identify this story as an example of a folktale? **GENRE**

2. What does Chimidyue think about weaving baskets before her adventure? How does being in a different place change her experience of weaving baskets? **THEME**

3. What does the word *different* mean on page 13? Use context clues to figure out the meaning. Explain how the root word *differ* helped you. **ROOT WORDS**

4. Write about the message the author communicates by having Chimidyue go into the forest. How was the forest different from what she imagined? What lessons did she learn? **WRITE ABOUT READING**

Compare Texts
Read about a cunning fox who taught a crow a lesson about vanity.

THE FOX AND THE CROW

Fox was sloping home tired and hungry. He'd been attempting to catch a mouse, but it kept darting away. The same thing had happened earlier when Fox had tried to catch a rabbit. It just wasn't his day.

Suddenly he spied Crow in the treetops with a large chunk of pale, creamy cheese in her beak.

"My luck is about to change," he thought. "Crow spends half her life admiring herself, so if I say she looks lovely, she'll talk to me and drop her cheese."

Fox stood just under Crow's branch. "Hello, Crow!" he called.

Crow was so surprised she nearly lost her balance. She glared at Fox.

"I was just admiring your beautiful, iridescent wings," said Fox.

"He's flattering me so that I'll drop my cheese!" thought Crow.

17

Crow didn't say anything, but she was pleased all the same and flapped her wings to show Fox that she'd understood.

"I can't let on that I'm noticing her actions," thought Fox, "because that will spoil my plan. If I keep complimenting her, she's sure to forget about the cheese sooner or later and will reply."

"Look how symmetrical your tail feathers are!" continued Fox. "I'd never noticed that they're like mirror images of each other!"

Crow had to admit that she'd never noticed that either. Being careful not to open her beak, she turned around to take a look.

"This isn't working yet," thought Fox, "but I'll keep trying. They don't call birds 'birdbrained' for nothing!"

"Those legs of yours must be just perfect for perching," Fox said slyly. "How did they become so strong and muscular?"

Keeping her beak firmly clamped on the cheese, Crow gazed down at her legs.

"They are strong, aren't they?" she thought. "I'd love to tell Fox their strength is from all my takeoffs and landings, but I can't, or I'll lose my meal."

"I think she realizes what I'm up to," thought Fox, "but I'll have one more attempt. If I don't get something to eat, I'm going to have a miserable night."

Fox studied Crow from head to claws, racking his brain for another compliment, when he saw something that he'd never noticed before.

"Do you know that your most beautiful feature is the bristles on your nostrils?" asked Fox.

Crow was overcome that Fox was paying her such close attention! Without thinking, Crow replied, "Thank you, Fox, for your wonderful compliments!"

The moment Crow spoke, the chunk of pale, creamy cheese fell from her beak straight into Fox's waiting mouth. With a lip-smacking gulp, he swallowed the cheese.

"Fox!" cried Crow. "You tricked me!"

"I did," replied Fox. "You really are beautiful, Crow," he called back over his shoulder, "but you're also birdbrained!"

Make Connections

What is the message in *The Fox and the Crow*?
ESSENTIAL QUESTION

Compare Chimidyue with Crow. What can we learn from each of them? **TEXT TO TEXT**

Focus on Literary Elements

Imagery Imagery is descriptive language that helps us make pictures in our minds. A writer uses imagery to describe how something looks, sounds, smells, feels, or tastes. We use these images to help us understand a story better.

Read and Find On page 4 of *The Wings of the Butterfly*, Chimidyue "quietly padded after" the butterfly. The description of the way she followed it paints an image, or picture, in our mind. We can see her walking quietly, carefully, and sneakily, as if she has padded feet like a cat. On page 6, her heart "beat more loudly than the birdsong." A rain forest is filled with the sounds of thousands of birds, so we can hear her heart pounding loud and hard.

Your Turn

Choose a character, place, or event in *The Wings of the Butterfly* and use imagery to describe it vividly. Write down your description, and then read it aloud to someone in your group.